Fact Finders®
INVENT IT

ZOOM IT

INVENT NEW MACHINES THAT MOVE

by Tammy Enz

Project Consultant
Daniel Enz, P.E., PhD
Assistant Professor, General Engineering
University of Wisconsin, Platteville

CAPSTONE PRESS
a capstone imprint

Fact Finders are published by Capstone Press,
1710 Roe Crest Drive, North Mankato, Minnesota 56003
www.capstonepub.com

 Books published by Capstone Press are manufactured with paper
containing at least 10 percent post-consumer waste.

Library of Congress Cataloging-in-Publication Data
Enz, Tammy.
  Zoom it : invent new machines that move / by Tammy Enz.
      p. cm.—(Fact finders. invent it)
  Includes bibliographical references and index.
  Summary: "Explains the principles of inventing and provides photo-illustrated instructions for making
a variety of moving contraptions"—Provided by publisher.
  ISBN 978-1-4296-7634-2 (library binding)
  ISBN 978-1-4296-7984-8 (paperback)
  1. Simple machines—Experiments—Juvenile literature. 2. Aerospace engineering—Juvenile literature.
3. Mechanical engineering—Juvenile literature. I. Title. II. Series.
  TJ147.E59 2012
  629.04—dc23   2011028739

Editorial Credits
Christopher L. Harbo, editor; Sarah Bennett, designer; Eric Gohl, media researcher; Marcy Morin,
      scheduler; Sarah Schuette, photo stylist; Laura Manthe, production specialist

Photo Credits
Capstone Studio: Karon Dubke, all cover and interior project photos
iStockphoto: Michael Braun, 27 (bottom), Steven Wynn, 22 (bottom left)
Library of Congress: 15 (bottom)
Shutterstock: Rich Carey, 8 (bottom left)

Design Elements
Shutterstock: alekup, liskus, Sylverarts, Tropinina Olga

Printed in the United States of America in North Mankato, Minnesota.
032012   006665R

CONTENTS

DRIVEN TO INVENT

People have been inventing new ways to move things for thousands of years. They've come up with wheels, airplanes, cars, and thousands of other inventions. All of these machines started when someone asked a question. Questions led to ideas. Ideas led to inventions. Sometimes these inventions worked. Most times they didn't. Inventors often need many years and hundreds of attempts to make their machines work. But the process of inventing is always filled with fun.

THE SIX STEPS OF INVENTING

Engineers and inventors follow a certain method when inventing. This method helps them build on their successes and learn from their failures. Inventors call the method's steps by different names, but the basics are always the same. Follow these six steps to see how inventing works:

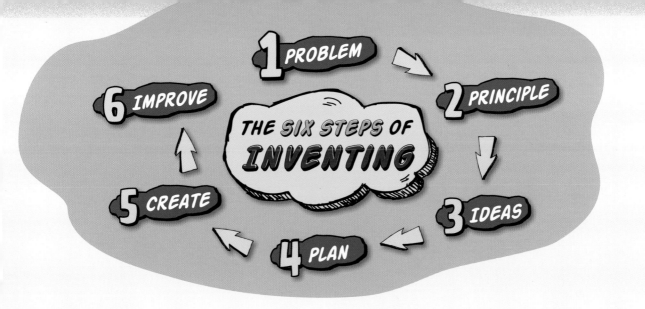

1 PROBLEM Inventors usually start with a problem. Ask yourself—What problem am I trying to solve?

2 PRINCIPLE Principles are basic rules or laws for how things work. Gravity is a principle that explains why a ball falls when you drop it. Friction is a principle that slows a ball down when you roll it across the floor. Ask yourself—What rules or laws apply to the problem I'm trying to solve?

3 IDEAS Write down some ideas that could help solve your problem. Be creative. Then pick the idea you think will work the best.

4 PLAN Plan how to build your device. Gather the tools and supplies needed.

5 CREATE Put everything together and make something new.

6 IMPROVE Once the solution is created, ask yourself if it solved the problem. If not, what can you change? If so, how can you make it better?

For each invention you build, the process starts all over again. Let's see these six steps in action with the inventions in this book.

CLIMBING SPIDER

1 PROBLEM Sliding a toy down a string is easy. Just hook it on and let go. Can you make something that climbs a string instead?

2 PRINCIPLE What principle helps things climb? Friction. Friction is the gripping force that prevents objects from slipping. Friction helps your sneakers grip the floor. It also helps people climb mountains.

3 IDEAS The rougher and tighter two surfaces are when they rub together, the more friction they create. Think of ways to use rough surfaces, sharp edges, or tight grips to make a spider climb.

4 PLAN

Gather together:
- ✔ scissors
- ✔ cereal box
- ✔ black marker
- ✔ ruler
- ✔ clear tape
- ✔ 2 1-inch (2.5-centimeters) long pieces of a drinking straw
- ✔ adhesive hook
- ✔ string

friction—a force produced when two objects rub against each other; friction slows down objects

1 Use a scissors to cut the back off a cereal box. Draw a spider on the blank side of the cardboard with the black marker. Make the spider about 3 inches (8 cm) wide by 4 inches (10 cm) long.

2 Cut out the spider. Leave the front legs connected to each other.

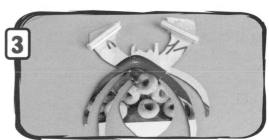

3 Tape the straw pieces to the spider's front legs. Angle the straws at about 45 degrees.

4 Stick an adhesive hook high up on the wall.

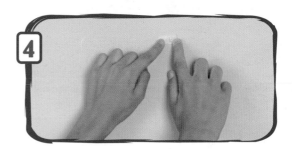

5 Run a length of string from the floor, up and over the adhesive hook, and back down to the floor.

CONTINUED ON NEXT PAGE ➡

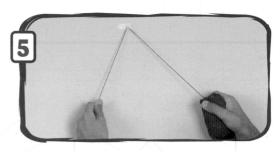

6 Cut the string. The two sides of the string should be the same length.

7 Thread the ends of the string through the straws on the spider's legs.

8 Pull one string at a time. Watch your spider climb.

6 IMPROVE

Did your spider shimmy up the string? Can you improve your invention to make the spider climb faster? Can you invent a way to make an action figure climb the string?

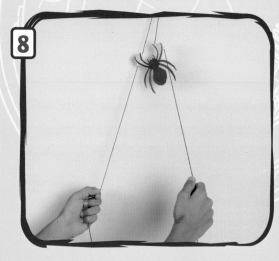

➡ ANIMAL INSPIRATION

In 2000 some Olympic swimmers wanted a swimsuit to help them swim fast like sharks. So the Speedo Company studied the secret to a shark's speed. They learned that sharks have tiny teeth called denticles all over their bodies. The denticles reduce drag on the shark's body. Speedo invented a fabric with tiny v-shaped ridges on it to mimic these denticles. The design was a great success. Most of the swimmers who won medals in the 2000 Olympics wore the new shark-inspired suits.

GAS-POWERED BOAT

1 PROBLEM Cruising around a lake in a motorboat is a blast! Can you build a miniature boat that propels itself across water?

2 PRINCIPLE Certain chemical reactions produce large amounts of bubbling gas. This gas can be captured and used to power a boat.

3 IDEAS A chemical reaction can be made in several ways. Mixing vinegar and baking soda releases a lot of carbon dioxide gas. Mixing effervescent tablets and water also produces this gas. Try out one of these reactions.

4 PLAN

Gather together:
- ✔ small plastic medicine bottle
- ✔ 2-inch (5-cm) long framing nail
- ✔ hammer
- ✔ needle-nose pliers
- ✔ bendable straw
- ✔ metal sardine can
- ✔ effervescent tablet

chemical reaction—a process in which one or more substances are made into a new substance or substances
effervescent—something that produces small bubbles

CONTINUED ON NEXT PAGE →

1 Place the bottle on its side and position the nail near its top. With an adult's help, use the hammer to carefully punch through the bottle's side. Remove the nail.

2 Use the pliers to carefully enlarge the hole made in step 1. Make the hole large enough to fit the straw tightly.

3 Slide the short end of the straw into the hole.

4 Place the bottle inside the can. Set the can in a pool or tub of water. Adjust the long end of the straw so it extends under the water.

5 Lift the bottle and straw out of the can. Fill the bottle about half full of water.

6 Break the effervescent tablet in half. Drop one of the halves into the bottle.

7 Quickly place the lid on the bottle. Place the bottle back in the can and reposition the long end of the straw in the water. Watch as gas bubbles push the boat across the water.

Does your boat glide across the water? Can you make it move faster? Can you make it bigger? Try other chemical reactions, such as baking soda and vinegar, to power your boat.

CONFETTI CANNON

1 PROBLEM You have a birthday coming up and want to use confetti to add to the excitement. Can you invent something that blasts confetti into the air?

2 PRINCIPLE Pressure is the principle that makes a cannon fire. Building up pressure inside a cannon causes a great release of energy when it fires. This energy makes a cannonball fly fast and far.

3 IDEAS A spark produces pressure. Compressed air also produces pressure. You can fire a confetti cannon if you find a way to compress air.

4 PLAN

Gather together:
- ruler
- 24-inch (61-cm) long by ¾-inch (2-cm) thick wooden dowel
- pencil
- utility knife
- 2 foam corks
- 2-inch (5-cm) long screw
- screwdriver
- 10-inch (25-cm) long by ¾-inch (2-cm) thick PVC pipe
- electrical tape
- 2 10-inch (25-cm) long pieces of string
- paper confetti
- stapler

> **pressure**—a force that pushes on something

12

1 Use a ruler to measure 1½ inches (4 cm) from one end of the dowel. Mark this spot with a pencil.

2 Place your ruler on the mark made in step 1. Measure 7 inches (18 cm) further along the dowel. Mark this spot with a pencil.

3 Have an adult use the utility knife to cut about ¼ inch (6 millimeters) off one end of one cork.

4 Center the cork circle on the end of the dowel closest to the mark made in step 1. Screw the wood screw through the center of the cork and into the dowel with a screwdriver.

5 Insert the end of the dowel with the cork into the PVC pipe. Slowly pump the dowel back and forth until it moves smoothly, but remains tight.

CONTINUED ON NEXT PAGE ➡

6 Pull the dowel out so that the mark made in step 1 lines up with the end of the pipe. Tape the end of one piece of string to the end of the pipe.

7 Stretch the other end of the string to the mark made in step 2. Tape this end of the string to the dowel at this mark. This string keeps the dowel from sliding out of the cannon when it's fired.

8 Drop a handful of confetti in the open end of the cannon.

9 Wedge the other cork into the open end of the cannon.

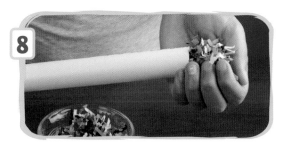

10 Staple one end of the other string to the end of the cork. Tape the other end of the string to the pipe. This string keeps the cork from flying across the room when you fire the cannon.

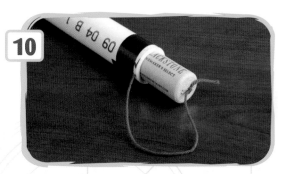

11 Point the cannon away from people or animals. Quickly push the dowel toward the cork. With a loud bang, confetti will explode into the air!

6 IMPROVE

Did confetti fly? Experiment with how much confetti to use. What else can you shoot with this cannon?

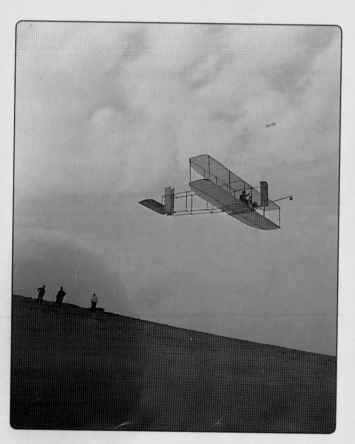

➡ CELEBRATE THE SMALL SUCCESSES

Wilbur and Orville Wright wanted to invent an airplane. They spent years experimenting. Finally in 1903 they were ready to try out their first airplane. Their airplane rose 10 feet (3 meters) in the air and stayed up for 12 seconds. Some people would have been disappointed. The Wrights considered it a success.

ELECTRIC CAR

1 PROBLEM
Pushing a toy car around gets old in a hurry. Can you invent a toy car that runs on an electric motor?

2 PRINCIPLE
A car with an electric motor uses gears to transfer power from the engine to the wheels. The arrangement of the gears determines how much power and speed the car will have.

3 IDEAS
You can use almost anything to make the body and axles of a car. Try balsa wood, cardboard, or plastic construction blocks. The key is finding a way to transfer power from the engine to one of the axles. Here is one design to try.

4 PLAN
Gather together:
- ✔ ruler
- ✔ 2 pieces of 4-inch (10-cm) long electrical wire
- ✔ wire stripper
- ✔ 1.5 volt DC motor
- ✔ electrical tape
- ✔ AA battery
- ✔ brass fastener
- ✔ ½-inch (1.3-cm) plastic gear
- ✔ 2 wood skewers
- ✔ pencil
- ✔ scissors
- ✔ sandpaper
- ✔ 4 1-inch (2.5-cm) plastic gears
- ✔ 3-inch (8-cm) square piece of corrugated cardboard

gear—a toothed wheel that fits into another toothed wheel; gears can change the direction of a force or can transfer power

1 Remove about 1 inch (2.5 cm) of plastic coating from the ends of each wire with the wire stripper.

2 Twist one end of each wire around a terminal on the motor.

TERMINAL

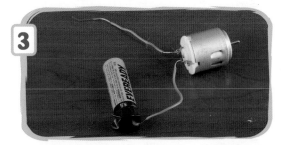

3 Tape the loose end of one wire to the positive (+) end of the battery.

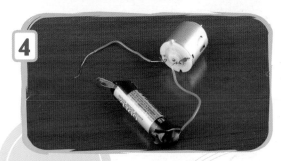

4 Tape the button of the brass fastener to the negative (–) end of the battery. Open the fastener's ends slightly.

5 Bend the loose end of the remaining wire into a hook. Carefully place this hook over one of the fastener ends to start the motor. Remove the hook to switch off the motor.

CONTINUED ON NEXT PAGE ➡

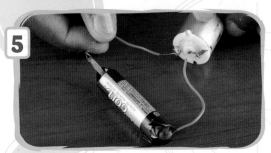

6 Slide a small gear onto the motor shaft.

7 Use a ruler to measure 3¾ inches (9.5 cm) from one end of a skewer. Mark this spot with the pencil. Repeat this step with the second skewer.

8 Use a scissors to cut each skewer at the marks made in step 7.

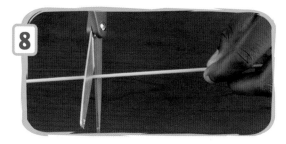

9 Carefully sand the ends of the skewers to points that fit tightly into the holes in the gears.

10 Slide one skewer through a hole between the layers of cardboard. The skewer should be about ½ inch (1 cm) from one end of the cardboard. Slide the other skewer through a hole about ½ inch (1 cm) from the other end of the cardboard. These are the axles.

11 Slide a large gear onto the ends of each skewer to make the wheels.

12 Position the motor on the cardboard. The small gear on the motor should connect with the large gear of one of the wheels. Tape the motor and battery to the cardboard.

13 Place the hooked wire over the fastener ends to switch on the motor.

6 IMPROVE

Did your electric car scoot across the floor? If not, make sure the axles can move freely. Adjust the position of the motor so the gears s___ contact. Try different size ___ the motor and axles to __ he car go slower or faster.

CATAPULT

1 PROBLEM You have two toy armies ready to battle, but you want to attack from afar. Can you invent something to add some action to your war games?

2 PRINCIPLE A catapult uses a spring to store energy that is then released to fling an object. The energy stored in the spring when it is squeezed is called *potential energy*. When the spring is released, the stored energy becomes *kinetic energy*.

3 IDEAS Any material that bounces back when you push and release it is a spring. A stiff piece of metal, a coil of wire, even a rubber ball can make a spring. Try using the spring from a clothespin for this project.

4 PLAN

Gather together:
- ✔ wooden clothespin
- ✔ 12-inch (30-cm) long 2x4 board
- ✔ 2 small trim nails
- ✔ hammer
- ✔ ruler
- ✔ wooden craft stick
- ✔ pencil
- ✔ utility knife
- ✔ hot glue gun and glue
- ✔ metal soda cap
- ✔ small ball

potential energy—the stored energy of an object that is raised, stretched, or squeezed

kinetic energy—the energy of a moving object

1 Remove one half of the clothespin from the spring and discard it.

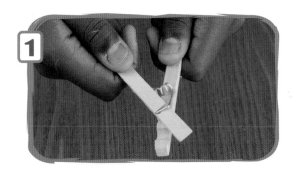

2 Remove the spring on the remaining half of the clothespin. Turn the spring around and place it backward on the clothespin.

3 Center the flat side of the clothespin on the board. With an adult's help, nail the clothespin into place with the hammer and a nail near each end.

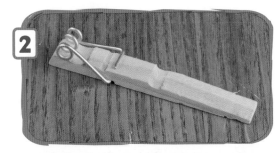

4 Use a ruler to measure ½ inch (1 cm) from the end of the craft stick. Mark this spot with a pencil.

5 Ask an adult to use the utility knife to carefully carve a small notch along the mark made in step 4.

CONTINUED ON NEXT PAGE ➡

6 Slide the craft stick into place so the notch is under the spring.

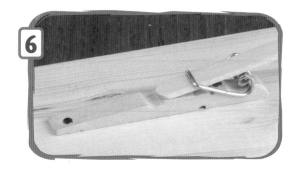

7 Hot glue the soda cap to the other end of the craft stick. Leave the last ¼ inch (.6 cm) of the stick showing so you can push on it.

8 Place a small ball in the cap. Push the stick down as far as possible. Release the stick to send the ball flying!

6 IMPROVE

How well does your catapult work? Try using a longer craft stick. Try letting the stick hang over the edge of the board so you can push it down farther. How far can you make the ball fly?

➡ SEE POSSIBILITIES IN EVERYTHING

Leonardo da Vinci is considered one of the world's greatest inventors. He was also an artist, philosopher, architect, designer, engineer, and scientist. Leonardo used many proven engineering principles. But he used them in new and different ways. Some of his inventions were unheard of in his day. He came up with designs for a bicycle, a glider, a helicopter, and shoes for walking on water. All around him he saw ideas for inventions.

WATER SHOES

CONTINUED ON NEXT PAGE →

1 PROBLEM You can walk on land. You can even walk on ice. But walking on water will take some special shoes. Can you invent a pair of shoes that allow you to walk on the surface of shallow water?

2 PRINCIPLE Buoyancy is the principle that describes why objects float. Objects float when they displace an amount of water equal to their own weight. The more you spread out your weight on water, the better chance you have of floating.

3 IDEAS Think of ways to spread out your weight on water. Can you connect bottles full of air to your feet? Maybe large pieces of foam could spread out your weight and help you float.

buoyancy—a natural phenomenon occurring when a submerged object is less dense than the water and is pushed up by water pressure, making it float

4 PLAN

Gather together:
- ✔ 2 3-inch (8-cm) thick, 6-foot (1.8-m) by 1-foot (.3-m) foam insulation boards
- ✔ tape measure
- ✔ marker
- ✔ coping saw
- ✔ utility knife
- ✔ 2-liter soda bottle
- ✔ scissors
- ✔ hot glue gun and glue
- ✔ duct tape
- ✔ 4 16-ounce plastic cups
- ✔ 2 broomsticks
- ✔ 2 milk jugs

23

CREATE

1 Lay a foam piece vertically on the floor. Use the tape measure to measure 6 inches (15 cm) over and 6 inches (15 cm) down from both of the top corners. Mark these spots with the marker.

2 Draw lines to connect the marks from step 1. You will create a point at the top of the foam. Ask an adult to use the coping saw to cut along these lines.

3 With an adult's help, use the utility knife to carefully cut off the top portion of the soda bottle. Discard the top.

4 Ask an adult to use the coping saw to carefully cut the bottle in half lengthwise. Each half will be a foot holder.

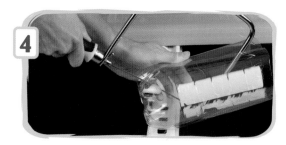

5 Place one half of the bottle over your foot. Use a marker to draw an arc where the top of your foot meets the edge of the bottle.

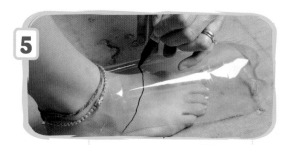

6 Use a scissors to cut out the small arc you drew in step 5. If the arc feels sharp, cover it with a piece of duct tape.

7 Measure down 3 feet (0.9 m) from the point created in step 2 to find the center of the shoe. Make a mark at this spot.

8 Hot glue the foot holder so it is centered on this spot. The foot holder should allow your toes to face toward the foam's point.

9 Wrap a piece of duct tape over the foot holder. Wrap its ends around to the other side of the shoe.

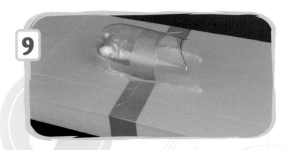

10 Turn the foam piece over. Cut two of the cups in half lengthwise with a scissors. Glue them to the bottom of the shoe in an alternating pattern.

CONTINUED ON NEXT PAGE →

11 Place a strip of duct tape over each cup to hold them in place.

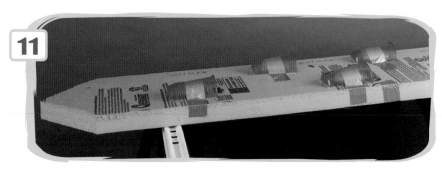

12 Repeat steps 1–11 with the other piece of foam.

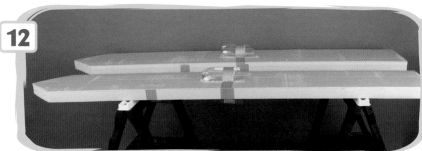

13 To make a support pole, stick the end of a broomstick inside the top of a milk jug. Tape the broomstick in place.

14 Repeat step 13 to make another support pole.

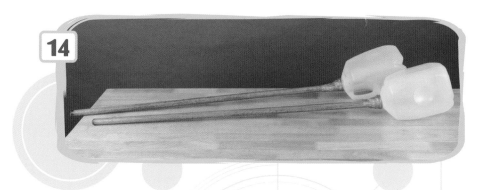

15 Take your shoes and poles to a shallow pool or pond. Make sure an adult is supervising. See if you can walk on water!

15

Can you walk on water? How far could you walk? If you weigh more than 100 pounds (45 kilograms), you may need thicker shoes. Try two layers of foam board. Also try using other materials that float. Can you make shoes with small plastic bottles?

➡ PASSION BREEDS SUCCESS

American Ralph Samuelson was a daredevil. He loved snow skiing. He wanted to find a way to ski on water. In 1922 no one had heard of such a thing. People laughed as he tried out his snow skis on the water. Then he tried skiing with some slats from a barrel. People were still laughing. But when he finally carved his own skis from a pine board, people stopped laughing. Ralph had invented a favorite summer sport—waterskiing.

SOAP BOAT

1 PROBLEM Boats are usually powered by wind or gasoline. But can you invent a boat that is powered by something really unique?

2 PRINCIPLE If you look closely at the surface of water, it seems to have a thin skin on it. This principle is called **surface tension**. It is caused by water **molecules** clinging to each other. Disturbing the molecules releases the tension. Releasing tension in one place causes the remaining tension to pull an object in the opposite direction.

3 IDEAS What are some ways to break surface tension? Oil and soap are two substances which disturb this tension. Try using soap to power a boat.

4 PLAN

Gather together:
- ✔ scissors
- ✔ 3-inch (8-cm) x 4½-inch (11.5 cm) piece of thin balsa wood
- ✔ utility knife
- ✔ toothpick
- ✔ 2-inch (5-cm) square piece of paper
- ✔ hot glue gun and glue
- ✔ bar soap

surface tension—a pulling force on the top film of a liquid
molecule—the atoms making up the smallest unit of a substance

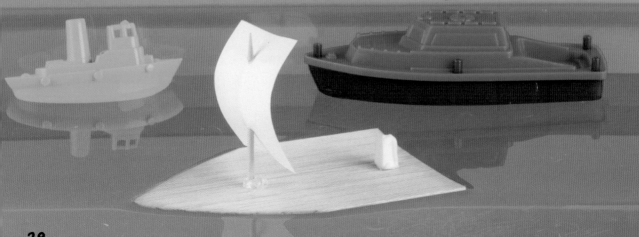

1 Use the scissors to cut the piece of balsa wood into an arched shape.

2 Have an adult use the utility knife to carefully cut a ¼-inch (.6-cm) square near the back of the boat.

3 Use the scissors to cut the sharp point from one end of the toothpick. Thread the small piece of paper onto the toothpick to make a sail. Hot glue the sail to the center of the boat.

4 Use a scissors to cut a small wedge of soap. Fit it tightly into the hole in the boat.

5 Place the boat into a tub of hot water. As the soap melts it will break the surface tension of the water. This action causes the boat to move in the opposite direction.

6 IMPROVE

Did your boat move forward? Are there other ways to move a boat by breaking surface tension? Try using a cotton ball soaked in oil or shampoo to power your boat.

GLOSSARY

buoyancy (BOI-uhn-see)—a natural phenomenon occurring when a submerged object is less dense than the water and is pushed up by water pressure, making it float

chemical reaction (KE-muh-kuhl ree-AK-shuhn)—a process in which one or more substances are made into a new substance or substances

drag (DRAG)—the force that resists the motion of an object moving through water

effervescent (ef-ur-VESS-uhnt)—something that produces small bubbles

friction (FRIK-shuhn)—a force produced when two objects rub against each other; friction slows down objects

gear (GEER)—a toothed wheel that fits into another toothed wheel; gears can change the direction of a force or can transfer power

kinetic energy (ki-NET-ik EN-ur-jee)—the energy of a moving object

molecule (MOL-uh-kyool)—the atoms making up the smallest unit of a substance

potential energy (puh-TEN-shuhl EN-ur-jee)—the stored energy of an object that is raised, stretched, or squeezed

pressure (PRESH-ur)—a force that pushes on something

surface tension (SUR-fiss TEN-shuhn)—a pulling force on the top film of a liquid

READ MORE

Bell-Rehwoldt, Sheri. *The Kids' Guide to Building Cool Stuff*. Kids' Guides. Mankato, Minn.: Capstone Press, 2009.

Enz, Tammy. *Build Your Own Car, Rocket, and Other Things That Go*. Build It Yourself. Mankato, Minn.: Capstone Press, 2011.

VanCleave, Janice. *Janice VanCleave's Engineering for Every Kid: Easy Activities that Make Learning Science Fun*. Science for Every Kid Series. San Francisco: Jossey-Bass, 2007.

INTERNET SITES

FactHound offers a safe, fun way to find Internet sites related to this book. All of the sites on FactHound have been researched by our staff.

Here's all you do:

Visit *www.facthound.com*

Type in this code: 9781429676342

Check out projects, games and lots more at
www.capstonekids.com

INDEX

ABOUT THE AUTHOR

Tammy Enz became a civil engineer because of her awe of the massive steel bridges that spanned the Mississippi River. She just had to figure out how they worked. Today, she still likes tinkering and figuring out how things work. When she isn't tinkering, she fixes up old houses and conducts experiments in her garden and kitchen. Most of all, she loves reading books about anything and everything and asking "why?"